The Weight of a Godly Woman

The Weight of a Godly Woman

Indigo Manning

LITTLE ROCK, ARKANSAS

The Weight of a Godly Woman
Copyright © 2021 by Indigo Manning

All rights reserved. No part of this book may be photocopied, reproduced, distributed, uploaded, or transmitted in any form or by any means, or stored in a database or retrieval system, without the prior written permission of the publisher.

J. Kenkade Publishing
6104 Forbing Rd
Little Rock, AR 72209
www.jkenkadepublishing.com
Facebook.com/jkenkadepublishing

J. Kenkade Publishing is a registered trademark.

Printed in the United States of America
ISBN 978-1-955186-02-5

Unless otherwise noted, scripture quotations are taken from the King James Version® Bible, Public Domain.
Used by permission. All rights reserved.

Scripture quotations marked NKJV are taken from the New King James Version® Bible, Copyright© 1982 by Thomas Nelson.
Used by permission. All rights reserved.

Scripture quotations marked NIV are taken from The Holy Bible, New International Version NIV® Copyright© 1973, 1978, 1984, 2011 by Biblica Inc™.
Used by permission. All rights reserved worldwide.

Scripture quotations marked ESV are taken from The ESV® Bible (The Holy Bible, English Standard Version®), copyright © 2001 by Crossway, a publishing ministry of Good News Publishers.
Used by permission. All rights reserved.

Scripture quotations marked NLT are taken from the Holy Bible, New Living Translation, copyright ©1996, 2004, 2015 by Tyndale House Foundation.
Used by permission of Tyndale House Publishers, Carol Stream, Illinois 60188. All rights reserved.

The views expressed in this book are those of the author and do not necessarily reflect the views of Publisher.

Dedication

I dedicate this book to my husband and sons. May you continue to push me and love me as we journey through this life together. Everything that I am today is credited to your love and support of me. I love you!

Table of Contents

Introduction..11
Chapter 1: Purpose..13
Chapter 2: Insecurities...................................23
Chapter 3: Identity..33
Chapter 4: Infertility......................................45
Chapter 5: The Wife......................................61
Chapter 6: Motherhood................................71
Chapter 7: Anxiety and Depression..............81
Chapter 8: Purpose in Betrayal.....................91
Chapter 9: Finding Her Again....................101
About the Author 111
About J. Kenkade Publishing 113

*Blessed is she who believed, for there will
be a fulfillment of those things
which were told her from the Lord.*

Luke 1:45 (NKJV)

INTRODUCTION

This book was inspired by all of the things I have faced and overcome in my life. I want to inspire and encourage the woman who is in a season of heaviness. Sometimes, this life can get hectic. It can feel like there is no way out. It can seem as if we have no hope for the future. The troubles of life can be suffocating. The good news is that we serve a God who cannot be defeated. He is sitting, waiting on you to take your load off yourself and onto Him. The weight of a godly woman was never meant to be carried by our fragile structures. Cast your cares on the Lord!

"For her worth is far above rubies..."
Proverbs 31:10 (NKJV)

PURPOSE

1: Purpose

There is something that should go ahead of us in all that we do, something that follows us everywhere we go. Everything we choose lies in this one thing. Every event that takes place in life works together for the sake of the full completion of this one thing. That thing is called purpose. We all have it. There is no escaping it. There is no way around it. We were created for it. God assigned it to us before we were formed in our mothers' wombs.

One thing about being a woman is that we give life.

There is a time in my life when I was very lost. Much of that was credited to the fact that I did not know or understand my purpose. If I am honest, I am still trying to figure it out in its full capacity. I do know that I am God's. I am His creation. Who better to consult about a thing than the Creator?

I have two children. The mother in me has this bad habit of getting them everything they want and even some of what I think they would want. When it comes to buying for them, I sadly do not limit myself (I certainly don't recommend that behavior to any mother). Anyway, they are little people, so a lot of what I buy them are toys. These toys typically don't come assembled, so I have to put them together or depend on my husband to do it. Well, if you have any experience with most men, they don't like to read things and follow instructions. They feel they are able to look at a picture and just put things together, and, well, they may be able to. That doesn't mean they will do it correctly.

That's sort of how we are with life.

We tend to cruise through, thinking, Well, whatever happens, happens, I have a whole life ahead of me. I have time to play then I can get serious.

That is such an unhealthy mindset for a woman with a purpose. When we truly understand what our purpose is, we don't leave room for nonsense. We don't toy around with our time. We don't waste time and energy on men who mean us no good. We don't lay with everything that compliments us. We don't invest our energy in relationships that bring no quality to our lives. We just don't!

You want to know how to truly live a full life? Find your purpose. The only way to do this is to seek God and ask Him to reveal to you the main reason you are here on Earth. He will answer you. He will guide you if you let Him. Now, living a life of purpose isn't easy. It isn't free. It isn't self-absorbed. Living a life of purpose requires sacrifice. It requires being completely sold out to God. One might ask, "What does that look like?" Well, contrary to popular belief, it looks like saying "no" to some of those girls' trips that you know will include some ungodly activities. It means changing your circle of friends and influence to reflect where you are trying to go and/or stay. It means letting go of some of the things that you enjoy most but really don't benefit you in the life you aspire to live.

There is a story in the Bible where a young man asks Jesus what he can do to have eternal life. Jesus replies by telling him he must follow His commandments. The young man tells Jesus that he has done all of those things. So, Jesus tells him, "There is one thing you haven't done. Go and sell all of your possessions and come follow me." The young man leaves sad because he is wealthy and does not want to give up his rich lifestyle for Jesus (Read Matthew 19:16-30).

You must be willing to let go of some things to truly follow God and pursue purpose. One of the things I used to love to do was play basketball with men. Most of the time, I was in what I considered to be a committed relationship, so it wasn't to scout a man or anything like that. It was just fun for me. I grew up in a house full of boys, and because I played sports, I would play with them and their friends all the time. When I was school age, this was beneficial for me because their they were more athletic than I was. There were a few times where that wasn't the case, but most of the time, it was. To play with boys who had better athletic capability made me better. It made my female competition seem small, mentally. It built character in me. It forced me to work hard. I truly enjoyed it. It was just fun. When I went off to college, I found other girls– well, now young women– like myself. There were, of course, girls who hung around and weren't into sports but just into the men. But me– I wanted to be on the court, shooting hoops with the fellas. What I began to realize was that this was the door to my dating experience. Almost every guy I dated was someone I met through sports. If it wasn't sports, it was church (but that's a different conversation for another chapter). When I realized this, I started analyzing my boundaries and the changes I needed to make if I wanted to get serious about pursuing my purpose.

I could no longer put myself in those environments. I met my husband, who was once my childhood best friend, through sports. I realize now, as a married woman, I cannot put myself in places I put myself in as a single woman. It just doesn't make sense. When it comes to being a woman of purpose, you cannot put yourself back in places that don't contribute to your purpose. Leave your Egypt and walk through your Exodus. Ask God to reveal your purpose and pursue it wholeheartedly until your time here is up. Don't leave room for distractions, though they are still going to come on their own. Be aware of the things you control. Remove yourself from people and environments that deter you from your purpose. Remember, women were created to give life. Anything you invest your time and energy inwto is what will thrive because you are giving life to it. If you invest in your purpose and pursuit thereof, you will not only have a full life, but you will also have the favor of God, and He will grace you for great things!

Let's Pray

Father God,

I thank You for life. I repent for my sins. Please forgive me. This life is precious to me, and I seek to live in a way that pleases You. I know that I can only please You by having faith, loving You, and loving others. That is the minimum that You ask of me. With a pure heart, I ask that You help me to commit to those things that concern You. I ask that You would reveal my purpose to me and give me clear direction in every area of my life so that I may serve You well. I open my heart to receive all that You have for me, and I am ready to fulfill my purpose on Earth.

I love You. Amen!

Ask God to reveal your purpose in life. What movements will you make to ensure you are living a full life, fulfilling the purpose of God?

INSECURITIES

2: Insecurities

All women face moments when we just do not feel one hundred percent. Maybe you look in the mirror and don't feel as pretty as you usually do. Maybe the outfit that you tried on and looked at thirty-five times yesterday just isn't the right outfit today. Maybe your bloat is a little more prominent today than it was two days ago. Maybe your skin doesn't seem as bright and luminous as it was before you went to sleep. We all have these moments; they're inevitable. The question is: how do we deal with them? Do we sulk in misery and set up the foundation for an entire day of dreadfulness? If we are honest, we know that many of us allow these very small details to set up a very "bad" day for us. I could credit it to the physical fluctuation of hormones, or I could talk about how our mental state makes all these things and some things that may not even really exist come to reality. It seems that we aren't even triggered; we don't even realize the imperfections until someone else comes along who we feel has it all, and then BOOM, we have an awakening. I'm not even sure it's fair to call it that. Hmm, maybe it's more like a slumber. I'm just saying, you have to be sleeping on yourself to feel that you are anything less than what God created you to be.

Every single woman on Earth has something that another woman wants. Maybe it's her drive, her nose, her lips, her intellect, her job, her car, her house, her perfect little kids, her fortune, or even her husband (what a sad case that is). Why do we always want what we can't have? Yeah, it's easy to go pay for a cosmetic operation or go find a job that is similar to the one she has or go get pregnant and have those babies or be the side chick. However, you still aren't getting what you really want out of those things: satisfaction and contentment. Going after what someone else has instead of accepting what God has for you only slows the process of your life. God has carefully orchestrated an entire plan and will for you. His plan always prevails, it never changes, and He never takes it away, but He will put it on pause and let you do what you feel you need to do to take control of your life.

See, God has a way of stepping back and saying, "You go, girl." He is that kind of gentleman, one who offers free will. Unlike many of the men we encounter, He has no desire to be controlling, leaving us with no choice but His own. No! God is all about decisions. I find it very funny that nsecurity literally means "the lack of confidence in oneself", yet we still try to find a way to control our own lives. Wow! How ironic! "I am willing to take matters into my own hands, even though I am not even sure of myself. But God, no. I don't want to let Him do stuff; He's just not working fast enough. He isn't making me happy. He doesn't give me everything that I want, so I have to get it for myself." We walk through life with the thought that we are not enough, but because of the many talents and strengths God created in women, we don't stop there. We find a way to make ourselves enough. We cake on makeup. We seek validation from empty sources. We allow partners to hurt us, be it physically, mentally, or emotionally, maybe even a blend of it all. We settle. We do all of this only to still feel insecure in the end. This is the healing for insecurities: trust God's plan for your life and don't allow yourself to fall into a comparison with anyone else. Look at another woman's life and say, "Aww, that is so good for her," and mean it. You will feel so much better about yourself. Talk to God, find out what He has for your life, and put all of your energy there. There is no point in wasting energy on someone else's life. Find security in Christ; it is sure to leave you confident in yourself as you stay in God.

Now, I only touched on one of the many areas of insecurity. Insecurity is also just simply not being motivated to do the things God has called you to do and being disobedient. Some of us have Moses spirits, or maybe they're Jonah spirits. Either way, we have doubted our abilities even though we know that God has told us to do something. I can raise my hand there. This book, and maybe even a couple more, should have been published a long time ago, but I doubted that I could even write enough to call it a book. I doubted that I would have enough content to discuss even though I find myself encouraging someone else or myself daily. I doubted that I would have the funds and resources needed to publish a book. I was so focused on the things I could see instead of focusing on what God told me to do. Believe me when I say that if God tells you to do something, He has already aligned the entire process and has provided every single thing you need even if you can't see it yet. He is that type of God. He is the ultimate Provider! Everything we need is in Him. We allow our insecurities or the areas we feel inadequate to hold us back. God called Moses to deliver the children of Israel out of bondage in Egypt. Moses didn't respond right away with a "yes". Do you want to know what he did? He presented his insecurity to God. Moses had a speech delay. So, when God told Moses to go and tell Pharoah to let His people go, Moses felt he was not capable of doing so.

Who are we to tell God, the One who created us, what we can and cannot do? It doesn't even make sense! If God tells you to do something, DO IT! (Exodus 3). Everything we need is in God. Jonah ran for so long, trying to escape from the calling on his life. All he did was make his life more difficult, and he went through tough times. I mean, he was swallowed by a whale, just to be spat out and do exactly what God told him to do from the start (Jonah 1).

Oh, you need to see an example of a woman who did this? Let's go with the one who started these shenanigans: Eve! Eve is the first woman to ever walk this Earth. Eve was so insecure. She had the perfect life! I mean perfect! She had the perfect body. She owned everything on Earth– literally. She had all the food you could eat. She was in power, alongside her husband, over every animal. She had a man who had eyes for her only. I mean, she was the only woman on Earth. There was no way he could cheat! She had everything! However, she felt the need to look for more. She was still insecure, and it led to the fall of mankind, and she was cursed because of it (Genesis 1-3). I say all of this to say: be secure in who you are. God created you just the way you are for a reason. You are unique. You are special. You are a gift to this world! Blot out all insecurities.

Let's Pray

Father God,

I am thankful that You took Your time creating me. I know that You love me and before You formed me in my mother's womb, You knew me. You knitted me together, and all that I am is Your work. I am fearfully and wonderfully made! I am beautiful, I am made in Your image, and I want to walk in my full potential knowing that You have all that I need. I repent for all my sins. Forgive me for being envious of others. I repent for procrastinating against Your orders. I ask that You forgive me for being disobedient to you and help me to move. I trust You, and I know that You will provide for me. Everything that I need is in You. You are my strength when I am weak.

I love You. Amen!

Take a look into your own life. What insecurities do you have? What steps will you take to break the barriers and walk in the power the Holy Spirit has given you to be whole in Christ?

_____
_____
_____
_____
_____
_____
_____
_____
_____
_____
_____
_____
_____
_____
_____
_____
_____
_____
_____
_____
_____
_____
_____

IDENTITY

3: Identity

I realized, in my many years of being lost, that I did not really know who I was. I try to reflect on when I was a little girl. I find it quite ironic that I do not remember myself as a little girl. As a little girl, I felt that I was a woman. Not by choice, of course. There were events that brought me into the threshold of womanhood far before I ever truly understood what it was. I will never understand why, but it seems to me that the world operates backwards. We grow inside our mother's wombs. The creation of another life comes from the deterioration of another. Every time a mother gives birth, she loses a part of her life. She loses flesh. She loses blood. She loses a piece of her. A piece that has grown inside of her, fed off of her, and developed from her inmost being is now a piece that will one day leave, never to return again.

When I look back at my childhood, all I see is an adult who was too big to stay inside such a little body. I used to wonder why I had to grow up so quickly. It never made sense to me. I wondered why things happened the way they did. I pride myself in never claiming to be the victim. Here I am, walking into my thirties, and I realized one day that I had absolutely no clue who I really am.

Ever since I was a young girl, I always looked up to my mother. I remember that now. My mother was a graceful woman. She left everything that she knew to be married. That led her into having three children by the age of twenty-five. I think about my life when I was twenty-five. I was still figuring things out for myself and the one child I had. At twenty-five, I had just decided to marry my now-husband. At twenty-five, I had just graduated college with my first degree. At twenty-five, I was preparing to move and start a new career in the military. At twenty-five, life– the life that I had dreamed of, anyway– was just beginning for me. But for her, it had already turned into something I don't think she planned at all. She was a mother of three small children with a husband. She was a stay-at-home mom, away from family and all that she knew in unfamiliar territory. I can only imagine how she felt. Overwhelmed, maybe. Tired. She put her dreams on hold, whatever they were. She lost herself in the everyday tasks of caring for others, as most mothers do. She, being very young when she married, didn't have much time at all to focus on finding herself in her adulthood.

I reflect on the little bit that I do know about my mother and the thoughts that were generated from on my own personal observation of her. I realize that I wanted to be more like her than

I thought. In many ways, I am like her. I grew up knowing that my mother was a caretaker. She has spent her entire life taking care of children. I ask myself: is that really what she wanted to do? Or is that something she settled for because she felt experienced after three children of her own? I went into the profession of childcare because it was what I saw my mother do for so many years. I recognized that. It became a part of my identity.

On the contrary, there were things about my mother I don't like that I started noticing about myself. My mother has always been really hard on me. Her approach to many things with me is controlling. She wanted me to do everything the way she would do it. She didn't leave much room for me to make my own decisions, though I did anyway. That dynamic– the fight in me and the need for control in her– caused severe tension between us when I was a teen. I have never liked to be "controlled". It only built a wall of defiance in me. It's funny I joined the military. In the military, everything you do is an order. You are told when to wake up, when to work out, when to eat, when to go to work, when to go home, and when to go to sleep. Everything you do is ordered by someone else. I ran from a certain thing and walked right back into it. Why? Because it became a part of my identity.

Not only did I run into the one thing I thought I was getting away from, but I became it. I often find myself trying to control everything around me. I realized I had a problem when I got married. Before marriage, I knew what I wanted my life to look like, but I didn't really understand that having a husband and children meant being open to others and their differences. I have to be willing to accept people as they are even if that means they don't fit into my bubble of reality. It also means that I cannot control every aspect of my life. I would be in a much healthier mental space if I could understand that I cannot control every little thing that happens in my life and that that is okay. Wanting to control everything around you leads to an unnecessary spiral of anxiety.

Here is the thing about our identities: our parents are and will always be part of us. Our parents are in us in some way. We do have the power to choose what parts of us we want to develop and what parts we want to suppress. We must be careful with this because oftentimes people spend so much time trying to convince themselves how they are different from their parent(s) or spend so much time trying not to be them that they actually become just like them. This is such an easy trap. From the time we are babies, we are shaped. A baby mimics everything they see and hear. Whatever their environment produces, the baby soaks up. It is scientifically proven that the most vital years of life are zero to three years of age. The reason is because the brain is still developing, and it soaks in everything that is being introduced to it. This is why it is inevitable for us to have characteristics like our parent(s). Then, there is the other side of biology called genetics. Some things are simply in our blood. Ever meet someone who acts like an absent parent or family member they have never met? Well, there you go! Genetics play a role in who we are as well, which leads me to my next and final point.

Every human being was created in the likeness of God.

God created us in His likeness (Genesis 1:17). This means that we are a reflection of God. We battle daily with our flesh because, well, thanks to our forebearers Adam and Eve, we were born into sin. However, when we are saved and receive the gift of salvation by confessing with our mouths that Jesus is the son of God and then we are baptized in the Holy Spirit, God's spirit is allowed to live in us. We receive His spirit. Therefore, our identity is in God. It is almost impossible to navigate this life as a believer without first knowing that every part of you belongs to God.

A woman who knows who she is in Christ is unstoppable. She is clothed in wisdom, she is full of knowledge, and she is confident in the

Holy Spirit. Your identity is only complete in God. You can stray away and try to be someone outside of God, and the only glory you will get out of that is worldly. That does us no good in the Kingdom. The Bible says, "What profits a man to gain the world and lose his soul?" (Mark 8:36). That means, "What good does it do us to have favor with people and work hard to please-people if God is not pleased?" We have no key to Heaven living that way. Our identity, every inch of our being must be in God.

God allows us to go through things in life. Those things shape us. They become a part of who we are. If we let Him guide and lead us through to the exit, we can go forward and pull others out because we already know the way. That is why we face trials and tribulations. We don't just go through troubles because God wants to watch us hurt. Some, if not most, of the problems we face are due to our own disobedience. We can't even think to blame God for that. But we serve a God who loves without condition. A God who takes every single thing in our lives and works it for the good of those who love Him, those who are called according to His purpose (Romans 8:28). That is why our identity has to be in Him.

We may be influenced by our surroundings; individual perspective is shaped by what we experience and see. We are a part of our parents and their parents because they are a part of our lives– our being. But we must recognize that our identity must be in God if we want His best for our lives.

Let's Pray

Father God,

We thank You for being the ultimate Creator. You took Your time and created me. You have kept me and guided me through some of the toughest times in my life. It is because of You that I am still here. In You, I have joy. In You, I am whole. I am grateful that I have a Father like You. Forgive me for all my sins. I repent and come before You, pure and humble. I ask that You would continue to reveal the things about me that need work and cultivate the things that are pleasing to You. I know that by grace, I am righteous. I present my body as a living sacrifice, holy and pleasing to You. Help me to live in my full identity in You.

I love You. Amen!

Who are you in Christ? Nothing else matters, you are who he says you are. What practical steps will you take to renew your mind daily and remind yourself who you are in God? How will you walk out this new life as a new creation?

_____
_____
_____
_____
_____
_____
_____
_____
_____
_____
_____
_____
_____
_____
_____
_____
_____
_____
_____
_____
_____
_____

INFERTILITY

4: Infertility

Who would have thought that I– a woman of so many talents, a mother, a wife, a child and faithful servant of Christ– would have this struggle? It seems that all I have ever prayed for, all that I have ever needed, and most of what I have wanted came with such speed and accuracy. Sometimes, the process takes longer than others or far more effort than others, yet it comes to pass. I remember before my first son was born that I dreamed of being a mother. For years, I made assumptions in my own mind of what motherhood would be like. The nurturing that I would give, the teachings that I would instill, the clothes that I would buy, the dinners that I would cook– it all came together so smoothly and so easily. I have known forever that being a mother was one of my assignments and that it would happen for me. I didn't know how soon or late, but I knew it would happen. Even as a young girl, I was always taking care of someone's child(ren). Not by force; I volunteered. I found myself to be a lot like my mother in this way. Initially, she was a stay-at-home mom. She raised three children during the day, all around eighteen months apart. How she did that daily

I am not the least bit sure. She had to have been almost completely insane by the time my youngest sibling started day school. Even then, he was still with her all day long, until he later went to kindergarten. I vaguely remember those events. I remember waking up extremely early in the morning so that she could go and open the center where she worked. It was a childcare center for low-income families. Sometimes, she would try to do my hair the night before so that it would already be done for the next day. Then, I recall seventy percent of the time, that didn't work out. Boy, was I a wild sleeper! This left me with the alternative: a series of flying ponytails and unmatched bows. My father did his very best. I look back at school pictures realizing what a horrific beautician he was. Sometimes, I would get a chance to go to work with Mom or attend events the center hosted or helped with. Those were always fun. Being her little helper was pretty fun, as well. Some of her coworkers had daughters who I would befriend and enjoy since I wasn't really used to much feminine company, growing up the only girl with no sisters and very few female cousins of local proximity. These memories are stored in the back of my mind, and I am reminded of my desire to be a mom. I am a mom. I will forever be a mother. Though I feel my parenting is short of perfection, I truly desired to share that with my husband. Before we got married, my husband had no children of his own, and though we tried and tried, it seemed that we would have no success getting pregnant. So we waited, and we waited, and we prayed. We found contentment with each new (unsuccessful) cycle.

I read a post on social media one day. It read: "People don't realize how insensitive it is to ask others why they haven't had children yet." I read that and immediately felt triggered. I think what caused more concern and alarm for me was that only minutes before I came across that, I witnessed a couple, friends of mine, approached in this manner. I don't feel the person meant any harm, but what I am sure was absent was the knowledge that this couple had also been struggling with fertility. We never know what people are going through. We must consider all things, be kind in our approach, and, most importantly, learn to mind our business. This journey really humbled me and taught me so much about myself and even more about God. I am not sure of His complete purpose for that journey; one day, it will all make sense. My major concerns, at this point, are catching the lesson and grasping the main points. I am certain it will be used as a tool at some point in my life to help, guide, love, and encourage others. It seems to be a much easier process to help others through something once you have been through it yourself. It's much more difficult to be on the outside looking in. It is almost impossible to lead on a dark path never taken. Only by way of God Himself can that be accomplished. I learned to listen to His voice and seek Him in my weakness and disappointment. Believe by faith only. The word of God had revealed something to me, and yet I waited on it. Waiting has to be one of the hardest things to do when you want something so badly. But in waiting, there are so many blessings, so much growth, so much opportunity, and so much dialogue between you and God. There is an open door for better relations with the King.

So, we waited.

We waited for His perfect plan to come to fruition. We did not allow our urge to interfere overpower our minds. We trusted God. We leaned on Him for strength in our weakness. We built a testimony to share with the world. Isn't that what this life is about? We live to be a model for this word, to see the revelation of His plan, His good and perfect will. Nothing more, nothing less. So, we waited.

So, it happened. We finally conceived! It was one of the happiest days of my life. To look at that test and see the two lines appear so rapidly was a fresh wind of clean, unfiltered air. I was so excited to share the news with my husband. I wanted to send him a photo through a text, but then I thought, How impersonal is that? I can't share such an intimate moment like this through the untouchable space of nonexistence. I have to tell him this in person. We have to have this moment together. I want to see his expression.

He will be so excited, I thought. He will be so happy!

I imagined all day how I would tell him. I imagined an explosion of fireworks in the sky, in our hearts, in our minds. I felt him sweep me off my feet and throw me in the air just to catch me as I came down. I felt the soft mush of his lips meeting mine as we sealed it all with a kiss and a prayer of thanks. For hours, I replayed the scene over and over in my mind. I could not wait for my husband to come home. Hours passed– minutes, seconds, milliseconds. The noise of my oldest son as he played echoed from one room to the next. The moment came where the click of the front door grabbed my attention as the sound screeched loudly in my ear. I ran to the door in excitement with a big smile on my face. I didn't think to ask how his day went. I wasn't concerned with the mood he was in. Nothing else in the world had my attention. I was zoned in on one person only: him. I grabbed him by his hand, and I led him into the bathroom where the lines lay resting on the bathroom counter. With a smile, I looked at it, then back at him. The look I received in return was nothing I had imagined. It was nothing that made me feel as though this was the climax I had so desperately awaited. The light in my eyes quickly dimmed into darkness as he stood there in confusion. I asked him what was wrong, and he proceeded to question the certainty of the image he had seen. I told him it was a positive test, the lines and that the lines meant we were pregnant.

It finally happened! What I didn't realize was that the pain from his past still haunted him. He couldn't allow himself to be excited or filled with joy. He couldn't process what had happened. He was paralyzed by the soil that buried him years ago, unable to breathe, unable to move, unable to see the life above the ground. I was always concerned about this. I wondered if it would affect him at any point in his life. I even asked him once if he ever thought about it? He told me no. He said he had instances where he thought, My child would be (insert age) this year, but that was as far as it went. I know him well, so deep down I could feel the curiosity that so deeply chased behind that statement. However, I forced myself to believe he was all right. That night, my heart was broken. I felt alone, once again. I felt this was no different than the last experience I had. Well, it was, but it wasn't. This time, it was planned, this time I was married to the love of my life. This time, we had sacrificed so much and prayed and hoped and supported each other through time after time of disappointment. This time, I had a companion. This time was different but not really. Though it seemed all the pieces matched together so well and the puzzle was complete, I realized I was missing the most important piece of them all: the picture. Imagine purchasing a puzzle from the store. You see a box that has a picture on it, a picture so tantalizing that you just have to have it. So, you buy it. You can't wait to get home to rip the plastic of the box, pour all the pieces out, and start the journey. Over the next few days, you work diligently, putting all the pieces together only to find that the picture you thought you were working toward isn't the picture you made. Someone put the wrong puzzle in the box.

That is the disappointment I felt that day.

Did he love me? Did he really want this? Why was he so passive in his response? Why did I feel so alone? Maybe this wasn't what we needed after all. Maybe, just maybe, this would ruin us. So many thoughts ran through my head that night, I could hardly think or sleep. I seemed to be in a space of blank disgust.

Well, time goes on. I went to work; so did he. I went to a church conference a few weeks later, and I had the most amazing time. I met people from all over the world. I saw young adults praise God like never before! I was so full there! The theme of the conference was "crazy faith". It was held in Tulsa, Oklahoma, at the new multi-million-dollar sanctuary of Transformation Church, led by Pastor Michael Todd. I was a part of history. Everything was great! I had given God so much praise while there. I praised Him for all He had done in my life, even more for the little baby I was finally carrying.

One day, in church, I was praising God, and He spoke to me, saying, "Do you love me enough to give it back to me?"

I gave a quick "Yes, God!"

I had no clue that in a couple of days, I would find out that I had lost the baby. I was at work in the middle of a field training exercise. I went to use the bathroom, and I noticed something wasn't right. I immediately ran to my commander and told her that I needed to go to the hospital to get checked out. Once I got to the hospital, I was told that I was threatening a miscarriage. I went home so worried, crying out to God to intervene so that I wouldn't lose this baby. Well, by the next day, the baby was gone. I had miscarried. I went on to have two more miscarriages. I had a total of three back-to-back. I felt lost. I felt like I was being punished for something. I felt like God was forsaking me. I was deeply depressed. My body was in pain. I was mentally exhausted. I was unemotional at this point. I was fighting to keep my faith, but deep down, I felt I had nothing to believe in at this point.

My husband didn't say much during this time, which made me feel like he just didn't care. I was angry with him. I felt alone. I felt like I had no support. This experience really affected our marriage. We struggled to see to each other's needs. Then, one day, I sat my husband down, and I told him that we needed to talk about it. We had been so passive and kept going through the motions and never really allowed ourselves to process what was happening. Before I knew it, my husband had broken down in tears. This was the first time in my life that I had seen him cry. I was so shocked and didn't initially know what to do or say. He expressed himself and let me know his concerns. This was the pivotal moment that shifted our marriage in this season. We supported each other, and we talked. We prayed together, and we agreed to just rest in God. Time went on, and we got better. One day, I had a doctor's appointment. The doctor had been running different tests to see if he could figure out why I wasn't able to hold my children. I went in, and I was going through the routines I always go through at my appointments. The first thing they do is give you a pregnancy test, then you go back out in the waiting room and wait to be called back. I was sitting in the waiting room when I heard my name. I gathered my things, and I began to walk into the back, following the nurse to my room. The nurse looked at my paperwork and told me to wait one moment and that she would be back. When she came back, she looked at me, and her face lit up. She told me, "Guess what, you're pregnant!" When I first heard her say it, I was quiet. I couldn't even be excited. The words were just what I wished to hear for so long, but the pain that I had gone through time and time again was still so fresh. Instead of being happy and excited to hear the news, I immediately began to worry. I asked so many questions about my bloodwork and my hormone levels. I was told I would come back to check all of those things the next week.

This was God!

We went on to have a successful pregnancy, and we now have another perfect little boy! The thing is, God was with us the whole time. We don't know why we had to go through the things we went through. We don't understand why it happened the way it did. What we do know is that God is a Promise-Keeper. The Bible tells us, "Blessed is the man who endures temptation; for when he has been approved, he will receive the crown of life which the Lord has promised to those who love Him" (James 1:12). God is pleased when we go through trials, yet we continue to trust and believe in Him. We struggled to keep going, we struggled to keep believing, but we never allowed our faith to waver. We knew that God promised us a son, so we knew that we would have one in His timing. God's timing is the perfect timing, that's for sure. He is pleased when we have faith in Him. In fact, it is impossible to please God without faith (Hebrews 11:6).

If there are any women out there who are struggling with infertility, I urge you to please seek God and His will for your life. Believe that He hears you, and He will give you the desires of your heart! His word says He withholds nothing good from those who walk uprightly. So, believe in His word and watch it come to pass. God is not the Author of confusion, and He does give us the desires of our hearts. Trust and believe, and He will see you through. Just like He did it for us, He will do it for you!

Let's Pray

Father God,

Thank You for always being there for me. Your word lets us know that trials will come but that if we remain steadfast in You, You will strengthen us, and we will be victorious. For this reason, I will give thanks in all circumstances! I will trust in the Lord with all my heart and lean not on my own understanding. Forgive me for letting my faith waver. I repent of all my complaints! Help me to keep my eyes on You when everything around me seems to look contrary to Your promises. I know that Your promises are "yes" and "amen". I believe God!

I love You. Amen!

God gave you a promise. Believe it! How will you exercise your faith and trust God during this season of your life?

THE WIFE

5: The Wife

Marriage is a beautiful thing. It was created to foster companionship and partnership. In Genesis, we see that God monitored His creations, and He saw Adam and said, "It is not good for the man to be alone; I will make a helper suitable for him" (Genesis 2:18, NIV). What is interesting about this verse is 1) He knew that man could not be healthy alone. He needed someone. We were not created to be alone. We need one another. 2) He made sure she was "suitable" for him. This means He created Eve with the idea that she needed to be a match for Adam. She needed to encompass everything he needed.

In the New Testament, we see that men and women need each other. One cannot be without the other. The Bible tells us that the woman is not independent of the man nor the man of the woman (I Corinthians 11:11, NIV). The sad thing is that society has convinced us that we do not need each other. I think we can all see the fruits of that misconception. Families are broken. Women are in the wrong positions. Men are not stepping up to the plate. Children are going haywire. The world is completely out of order. Life is completely out of control. That was not the way God intended for things to be, and that is why the life we know today is not the Eden God created in the beginning. As a wife, understand that you have a purpose. You have a calling. You have been equipped to be all that your husband needs. I know that sometimes that can be overwhelming. It can seem draining. It can feel like you are inadequate sometimes. Life isn't what it used to be for the traditional wife. In this day and age, wives are working full-time jobs, they are leaders outside the home, and they are coming home changing hats to be the cook, the maid, the counselor, the nurturer, the educator, the mediator, you name it.

Life is full for the modern-day wife, yet you still have a responsibility to be a wife. That can be hard. It can be taxing mentally, physically, and emotionally, but you are equipped. God made you "suitable". We have to make a conscious decision to wake up every morning and renew our minds and seek God for our assignment(s) for the day. When we make a habit of this, we receive the grace He so readily has available for us. When we do this, we are telling God, "I know I don't have all the answers, and I know I can't do this on my own, but I trust You to make me suitable today. I trust You to empower me to be all that I need to be today, in this moment. I trust you to complete me. God, I am a willing vessel, ready to be the wife you called me to be."

Believe me when I say, He will come through

for you. A wife is a blessing to a man. We know this because the word of God says, "He who finds a wife finds a good thing and obtains favor from the Lord." That's how special you are to God. God calls you a "good" thing. He gives favor to the man who finds you. He says you are His precious, delicate gift, and He wants to ensure your husband is responsible with you. He wants to be sure you are covered and protected. He wants to be sure you are well taken care of. He instructs the husband to love his bride as Christ loves the church. There is no greater love than this. Christ literally laid his life down for the sake of His bride (the Church). He expects nothing less of the husband.

No wife is expected to allow herself to be a victim of abuse or sexual immorality. Anyone who would feed you this inconsistent, non-biblical advice is wrong. That is not the guidance the Word of God gives us. The wife should be loved as Christ loves the church; if a man is not doing that and is making no effort to do so, he is not worthy of you. This is why we must be very careful with who we pledge our lives to. Marriage is a serious matter, and it is to be honored by all (Hebrews 13:4, NIV). So, remember: you are a prize. You are God's creation. You are to be held in high regard. You are your husband's first priority, and he is yours. Nothing but God comes before the two of you.

If you ever want to pull out the best version of your spouse, you have to walk out the Word of God. Make a conscious effort to always love as God instructs us. If we put our best foot forward in every situation, we are building the best version of ourselves while bringing out the best versions of our spouses. Like our children, we have to live by example in order to influence our spouses by works and not just by words. Our spouses will replicate our actions, so we should make an effort to only perform godly actions that will grow within both husbands and wives. Many times, women have a tendency to force things. We feel as if we have the power to make people who we want or need them to be, and that is just not the case. Honestly, it is counterproductive. No one wants to be demanded to do anything, especially a man. Men don't like to receive demands from each other, let alone women. That is just not the approach to take in marriage. It is not only unhealthy, but it is ultimately controlling and can or will make your husband feel belittled, which will cause him to shut down and be far less likely to receive anything you have to say.

One thing that I learned in marriage is that God can do far more changing than I can. God is a pro at transforming hearts. As long as someone is willing to change and become a better person, God will do the changing. The Bible says it is better to live in a corner of the housetop than in a house shared with a quarrelsome wife (Proverbs 21:9, ESV). In other words, all that nagging? Ain't nobody tryna hear that. Men do not hear that, anyway. All they hear is muffled yelling. This is why it is very important that you know your spouse. You must know how to communicate effectively and get through to him with gentleness and respect. Men need respect. They need to feel needed. They need to be held in high regard. They need their egos to be stroked. That is just who they are. They don't need their wives to try to control them and tell them what to do. I know that for some of us, this approach seems unproductive because men can also be very stubborn individuals. However, as I said before, God can reach him far better than you can. Pray and ask Him to intervene when things don't seem to be going the way you want or need them to. Speak life over your husband. Speak the things you want to see in him and don't give so much attention to the things you don't like about him. What we train our minds to focus on is what we will breathe in. If all you can see are his flaws, those are all you will ever see. If all you can focus on is what you don't have, you will miss out on all that you do.

Cherish what you have. Remember who you are. You chose to be his wife. Do all you can to be the best one you can be. You are suitable for him!

Let's Pray

Father God,

I thank You that You created me to be a helpmate. I thank You for my husband. I ask that You would continue to lead and guide me as I seek You for direction in my marriage. Help me to be selfless and put his needs before my own. Help me to be the wife that You ordained me to be. I know that my marriage is as strong as my efforts, and I ask that You continue to empower us to love each other the way You have instructed us to. We desire to keep You at the center of it all. As we allow You to lead, lead us through this life until death do us part.

We love You. Amen!

In what areas can you improve as a wife? What are your strengths? What goals do you wish to obtain in your marriage?

MOTHERHOOD

6: Motherhood

She watches over the affairs of her household and does not eat the bread of idleness. Her children arise and call her blessed...
Proverbs 31:27-28 (NIV)

There is such a gift in being a mother. Being a mother is something that should not be taken for granted, nor should it be handled lightly or without wisdom. The gift of motherhood is a privilege. It is a blessing from God. Not everyone woman gets to experience motherhood. Not every woman wants to experience motherhood, and that is perfectly okay. If you have been graced in this area of life, it is very important that you show up daily. Sometimes, it can be challenging. Some days, it is exhausting. Some days, it is the best feeling ever. Some days, we barely roll out of bed. Some days, we just want to be left alone. Some days, we cannot think of anything else. Motherhood is a sacrifice in itself. There is this notion that once our children turn eighteen years old, our job is done. The truth is, as mothers, our job is never complete. Jesus was a fully grown man, and Mary still saw to him. When he was being crucified, when he was being tortured, as innocent as he was, she was right there. Until death, you are still their mother, and it is your job to nurture, protect, teach, provide, and train them up in the way they should go.

Being a mother is full of adventure. It is full of challenges. It is a learning experience. Being a mother requires grace, patience, skill, intentionality, planning– it takes God. God knew we would need Him in this area of life, and that is why He made sure we had plenty of examples of good and bad in the Bible so that we could take from those experiences and use wisdom in our approaches to parenting.

I am a mother of two children. I have two boys ages seven months old and five years old. They are two totally different children, and they have totally different needs. I have to be able to look at my children as individual beings. I have to watch them as they grow and evolve. I have to make a conscious effort to get to know them as they develop into grown men. They have individual needs. This is pertinent to know and remember when it comes to raising children. Learn and understand and accept that they are their own beings. We must invest time into familiarizing ourselves with our children so that we can best meet their needs. My five-year-old no longer drinks from a bottle, and he no longer needs me to spoon-feed him. He is very capable of feeding himself and drinking from a regular cup. My seven-month-old son can hold his own bottle, but if I were to give him a regular cup, he would spill the contents everywhere, if not choke. He can't feed himself, so I have to sit and spoon-feed him to ensure he gets the nutrition he needs. This is an extreme example, but the point is that all children have their separate needs. We must assess them and learn what those needs are and how we can best meet them. Just like you and the person next to you have your own personal needs, so do your children. You can't take the same approach with multiple children.

Children need a healthy balance of discipline, instruction, and nurturing. They don't deserve to be victims of our pain, but how often does this happen? If I am honest, I have had days where work was very unpleasant, and I come home and am short-tempered and impatient with my son. I realize what I am doing, and I apologize to him. I explain to him that it was wrong for me to project my feelings on him. He had had absolutely nothing to do with that, and, most likely, he was only acting as a five-year-old boy typically acts. The mistake some parents make is that they feel they are always justified and that they are always right. Wrong! Just because you are an adult, it does not mean you are always right. Here is a huge tip: you can be wrong, too. The best thing to do is acknowledge those wrongs and genuinely apologize to your child(ren) when you make a mistake. Not only does this cultivate a healthy channel for communication between you, but it also teaches your children that mistakes are inevitable, and they will learn how to respond to mistakes in the process. As a mother, you are the first person your child will ever know. For a natural mother, this little being literally came from you. You have shared the same flesh. You have incubated this human for ten months. You have carried this child your entire life until the seed was fertilized, humanized, and birthed. For the spiritual or adoptive mother, you were ordained to mother this child from the very beginning. Your assignment is no different. Some of you may never naturally birth any children, but that doesn't mean you were not called to be a mother. Don't you think of yourself or your relationship with your children as any less. All of these tools and practical applications still apply to you. What we fail to realize is that our entire lives were ordained before we were ever born. God told Jeremiah, "I knew you before I formed you in your mother's womb. Before you were born I set you apart..." (Jeremiah 1:5, NLT). This lets us know that everything about our lives was planned before we ever came to be.

You were called to be that child's mother before it ever came to be. Whether or not you carried that child has absolutely nothing to do with how valued you are. There are women who carry children and aren't capable of being the mothers they probably wished to be. You are gifted, and you are graced to be a mother just as the next mama. Never let anyone tell you any differently. Ultimately, motherhood is a lifelong responsibility. It is a gift from God. Always pray over your child(ren). Always seek God regarding their wellbeing and yours. Make every decision under the unction of the Holy Spirit, and you can trust that you are doing your best by them. Sometimes, we put so much pressure on ourselves, and we self-sabotage. As long as you are giving your all, you are doing your very best by them!

You deserve to give yourself applause. Life as a mother is challenging, and it can come with many obstacles, but you were created to overcome them all. You are a child of God, and just as well as you take care of your children, He takes care of you. You must ensure that you are taking care of yourself. You must be intentional in seeking God every day to be equipped and prepared to do that well. God has everything you need. If you are tired, He will give you rest. If you are overwhelmed, He will take a load off. If you are incompetent, He will make you whole. You are a great mother! With God, nothing can ever defeat you. Keep pushing, mama!

Let's Pray

Father God,

I thank You for my child(ren). I thank You that You have graced me to be a mother. I hold this position in such a high regard, and I honestly want to be the best I can be for my child(ren). I ask that You would continue to lead and guide me in Your ways as I teach and guide my family. I love You, and I love the blessings You have entrusted to me. Help me to be the loving, kind, and wise mother I need to be in order to help my child(ren) grow and develop into Kingdom citizens. My child(ren) is a world changer/are world changers, and I know that You have ordained him/her/them to be a vessel/vessels for Your Kingdom. Reveal his/her/their purpose to me so that I may cultivate all he/she/they is/are called to be. Help me to make wise decisions. Help me to acknowledge when I am wrong. Help me to create healthy, lasting relationships with him/her/them that will defeat generational curses. Let nothing destroy the connection I have with my seed(s). As You father me, help me to parent my child(ren) well.

I love You. Amen!

What desires do you have for your children? What generational curses are you putting an end to? What goals and plans do you have for your children's futures?

ANXIETY AND DEPRESSION

7: Anxiety and Depression

Women have it hard in the areas of mental and emotional health. Why is that? Well, we have these things called hormones. They are so easily imbalanced, and it can cause a chain effect of problems. We are often called "crazy", "bipolar", "angry", "aggressive", and the list goes on. Many of these non-medical diagnoses are a reflection of our emotional beings. Women are typically very emotional. We can't help it! Anything can throw off our hormonal systems: nutritional and diet changes, childbirth, medications, the environment, stress, or life-altering events. The list is never-ending.

The question is: how do we process these things? And how do we overcome the issues that arise as a result of these things? The most common mental health problems many women face are depression and anxiety. These are two demons that haunt us all in some way in some capacity in our lives. The good news is that God has given us spiritual tools to apply to overcome and defeat them. The Bible tells us, "Be anxious for nothing, but in everything by prayer and supplication, with thanksgiving, let your requests be made known to God; and the peace of God, which surpasses all understanding, will guard your hearts and minds through Christ Jesus" (Philippians 4:6-7, NKJV). What God is telling us here is that we don't have to stay there. When these things creep up in our minds, we have the option to give them to God and allow Him to trade anxiety and depression for peace. To live a life full of peace is a desire of us all. I'm sure no one in their right mind wants to be tormented by mental instability. It isn't pleasant, and it isn't what God wants for us.

I struggle heavily with anxiety. Much of that comes from the need to control everything in my life. Whenever things seem to feel out of control, I tend to lose sight of the access I have to God, and it causes physical harm that doesn't have to be. Depression is a battle I fought when I went through sexual abuse and later in my journey of infertility. So, I can tell you firsthand that peace is so much easier and more comfortable to live in. Do not hold on to these things. Anxiety and depression could be heavy enough to kill you. Premature death isn't what God wants for any of us, and that is why He offers us a rescue plan. Cast your anxieties on Him because He cares (1 Peter 5:7, ESV). Now that we talked about the spiritual benefits, let's touch on the practical approach. God has given us the gifts of therapy and counseling. For some reason, these are tools that have been shamed for so many years.

Society once told us these things were not needed. We were told if we went to see a counselor or therapist, something was wrong with us. That is not true. These are healthy methods of recovery and healing that could be the answer to your problems. Many of us were not equipped with the right tools to handle these issues on our own. It is perfectly okay to find a professional who can help you work through your problems in life. Many of us are held hostage by past hurts in our lives, and we don't even realize it. Some of us were abused in our childhood, and some of us were surrounded by unhealthy relationships. Some of us were never nurtured well and have a hard time dealing with the turmoil of this life. Get help! Let no one convince you that seeking help makes you weak. Allowing yourself to drown in mental instability is weakness. Getting help is the most heroic thing you could do for yourself and the ones you love.

No one who truly cares for you wants to sit back and watch you suffer. No one who truly loves you will say anything belittling to you when you are already at your lowest point in life. Get the help you need to live the full life God wants for you. Life has enough problems of its own. The Bible permits us to seek wise counsel when we need it. It is foolish to wander blindly and aimlessly with no hope. Who wants to live a life like that? That's not living at all. Sister, I am advising you to get help and heal!

What does anxiety look like? What are the symptoms? Anxiety can appear in many different ways. Some physical symptoms could be (but are not limited to): headaches, stomach problems, rapid heartbeat, chest pains, shortness of breath, dizziness or lightheadedness, excessive sweating, lack of sleep, fatigue, menopausal symptoms, impaired immune system, constant paranoia, decreased libido, and many more. If you feel you are facing difficulties in life and you notice any of these symptoms are consistent, please seek help and get a diagnosis. Allow a professional to assess the issue, diagnose if necessary, and create a treatment plan to help you overcome anxiety.

What are signs of depression? Depression can be clinically diagnosed. It can be temporary. It can be long-term. It can be onset by many different things. One common type in women is post-partum depression, or "PPD". This comes during or after childbirth, and it can result in harm to the mother and/or her child. This disease or sickness must be monitored closely, and it is necessary to evaluate and assess all triggers and causes and seek help. Signs of depression can include but are not limited to isolation, loss of interest, feelings of hopelessness, suicidal thoughts, loss of appetite, risky behaviors, fatigue, lack of sleep, unexplained mood swings, and many more. If you are experiencing depression, please seek help. There is a professional somewhere waiting to help you assess your situation and come up with a treatment plan to help you discover a better you.

Let's Pray

Father God,

We recognize these attacks of the enemy. We thank You for discernment, and we thank You for the Holy Spirit. We know that where the Spirit is, there is liberty. We know You to be the Prince of Peace. We ask that You would help us utilize the tools You have given us to live lives of freedom. We desire to have renewed minds, free of depression and anxiety. We know that Your will is for us to live full lives of prosperity. Help us overcome these challenges. Lead us to the right sources who can help us gain the practical skills we need to apply and overcome these traps of the enemy. We trust that You will bring us through these difficult times.

We love You. Amen!

Are you struggling with anxiety and/or depression? Have you sought out help? What steps are you taking to heal and overcome this season in your life? What goals do you wish to set for yourself?

PURPOSE IN BETRAYAL

8: Purpose in Betrayal

*You have heard that it was said,
"Love your neighbor and hate your enemy."
But I tell you, love your enemies and pray for
those who persecute you, that you may be
children of your Father in heaven...
Matthew 5:43-45 (NIV)*

Many of us have faced some sort of pain in relationships. Some pain is more bearable than others, but, ultimately, it's still uncomfortable. In my experience, I have probably experienced every type of pain there is in relationships. I have been heartbroken in intimate relationships. I have overcome the abandonment of a parent. I have been outcast from family. I have been wronged by friends. I have been disrespected and belittled in professional settings. The list goes on. None of these things felt good. Some of them have required daily reminders to get up and make a decision that I would not be a victim. The best approach to dealing with betrayal in relationships I have taken is remembering who I have on my side, the One who will never leave me nor forsake me. I have God.

Far too often, we put unrealistic expectations on people who are just incapable of being who we expect them to be in our lives. Due to the trauma I have faced in familial relationships, I have always approached new relationships with caution. I have trust issues that I work through daily. This can be very daunting and unhealthy. I am sure you probably have similar convictions in your life as well. I am here to tell you it is essential that we learn to meet people where they are. We cannot continue to place unrealistic expectations on people and think we will live in perfect bliss. Betrayal is one heartwrenching thing, but if you are a victim of that, just know that it will all work together for your good. Let's take a look at how betrayal benefits mankind. Jesus walked the Earth, and He handpicked His disciples. He taught them. He loved them. He ate with them. He lived with them. He embraced them even though they were unworthy of His perfection. However, he was still betrayed.

The funny thing about Jesus' situation is that He knew it was coming. He even told His betrayer what would happen and when. He was aware of what would happen, and He still loved. The reason Jesus responded the way He did was because He knew it was necessary for His purpose. He knew the decisions that would be made would lead Him to the cross. He knew the cross was essential to my life and yours. I'm sure this didn't feel good in any way. We look at these things, and we think Jesus' life was so easy, but it was not. The way you and I feel when we are wronged by someone is the same way Jesus felt when it happened to Him, but He didn't sulk in it. He used it as a stepping stone to move forward.

I have been in situations where I confided in someone and everything I told them was used against me later. I have been asked for advice, and my words were later twisted into attack and judgement, taken totally out of context. I have watched the people I love spew hateful expressions at me for simply choosing to do what is right. I have been ignored and uninvited in instances where I just wanted to feel loved and included. I have been rejected by a parent who created me when I didn't ask to be here. I have been falsely accused at work. I have been belittled and had others' insecurities projected onto me because they were simply jealous of something I didn't even realize I had. I have dealt with infidelity. I have been physically and sexually abused. I have been taken advantage of.

We all have faced betrayal, and it certainly isn't pleasant. However, God is a God of comfort. He is the ultimate Healer. He can mend our hearts back together again after they have been ripped apart by the people we love most. There is no problem too big for Him. In the Psalms, we see where David was constantly pursued by his enemies, and he cried out to God. The crazy thing is that his enemy, Saul, was once a friend and an ally. His jealousy of the mighty grace David carried led him to rage and evil pursuit. He planned to take David's life so as to ensure he would not overtake his throne. Isn't that sad? Someone would be so jealous of you that they would do you harm. This is the life we live. That jealous spirit that Saul carried can make its way to us. It still lurks today. It is unfortunate, but it is real! The bigger issue here is knowing how to respond to these situations. How do we heal from this type of hurt? How do we make intentional decisions that will help us to overcome the effects of such treatment?

God is the answer.

The Bible gives us practical and spiritual tools to navigate through these unpleasant seasons of life. The main thing we don't want to do is retaliate or try to get even. We also don't want to hold grudges or allow these things to sit on our hearts and fester into ill feelings and actions that will make us accountable for wrongdoing. We must trust that God will fight our battles and that He will guide us through the process of recovery from this hurt. We know that His word tells us, "the Lord is nigh to them that are of a broken heart; and saveth such as be of a contrite spirit" (Psalm 34:18). This is so true on many levels. I am a witness. In my times of hurt and brokenheartedness, I have always gotten to a point where I just had to lean on God and sulk in His arms. He comforted me and brought me back to the wholeness that He so freely gives. As a result, I was not only healed and made whole again; he also gave me a renewed mind, and I came back stronger. I learned some things about myself. I rid myself of unnecessary burdens. I went forward in life with the newfound knowledge that my trust must only be in God, not in man. God never tells us to put our trust solely in man. He tells us to put our trust in Him and love man. When that trust is misplaced, we set ourselves up for failure. If God didn't tell you to trust someone, use wisdom in how you approach that relationship.

What we all can do is trust everyone to be exactly who they are. That doesn't mean we have to trust them with our vulnerability too freely. Understand that in this life, we will face disappointments. People won't always reciprocate the love we give. Some people in our lives are only there for a season. Others are an assignment. God should be the One who permits every connection in our lives. If we consult God in the very beginning, not only will we be aware of what is happening, but we will also know what to expect and how to navigate that relationship, and we will be protected in whatever is to come. The enemy can't catch you off guard when you are guarded by the Holy Spirit. Let Him heal you from past hurts. Let Him lead you from here on out. He will give you insight and foresight and equip you for every relationship you are ordained to enter!

The Lord himself will fight for you.
Just stay calm.
Exodus 14:14 (NLT)

Let's Pray

Father God,

Thank You for Your wise words of instruction. Thank You for being by my side when I am hurt and heartbroken. I find comfort in You. You rescue me from the snares of the enemy, and I am grateful. I pray that those who persecute me will first see the beauty in themselves and seek You. You are able to transform any heart that is given to You, and I ask that You work on my heart and theirs. You are a God of order, and You give me peace. For that, I worship You, and I honor Your presence. May Your Holy Spirit lead me and guide me in my relationships going forward. As I walk in my healing, help me to help someone else heal from past hurts.

We love You. Amen!

What pain have you been holding on to? Is there someone in your life you need to forgive? How can you make better decisions in your relationships going forward?

FINDING HER AGAIN

9: Finding Her Again

There are many virtuous and capable women in the world, but you surpass them all! Charm is deceptive, and beauty does not last; but a woman who fears the Lord will be greatly praised.
Proverbs 31:29-30 (NLT)

Life has a way of knocking us off our post. It is hard work being a woman of God. There is nothing accidental about who you are. The Bible tells us, "All things work together for the good of them who love the Lord, to them who are called according to his purpose" (Romans 8:28). God has ordained every single event that happens in our lives. Some of the things we go through are consequences of our own actions. Other things are simply part of life. Either way, we are not exempt from trials and tribulations. So much can happen over the course of life. Life events happen, and we can sometimes lose ourselves in the midst of it all. That little girl who was sitting in her room playing with her toys and imagining what her life would one day be is now a grown woman who carries all the baggage of life's experiences.

Many of us forget who we were before life happened. We get an education. We leave home.

We go out into the world. We get our hearts broken. We marry. We have children. We start careers. We start businesses. We evolve. Everything that happens in life comes back full circle. You have to find that girl again. Find the one who had dreams and ambitions. Find the girl who once had a simple life before it all happened. Find the pureness of that little girl who God covered and held in her innocence. Find her and remember who you are. Remember who you were before it all happened and break loose from the chains the enemy has tried to use to restrain you. Whom the Lord sets free is free indeed. You don't have to be held captive by all of the responsibilities of life. You don't have to stop dreaming. You don't have to stop building. Things may have paused. Things may have come to a halt. Things may have slowed down, but that was not the end. It isn't over until you give up.

You may have failed. So what?

Learn from that failure and do better next time. Maybe things didn't happen the way you planned them, but you still have breath, so guess what– there is still time. So, what? You didn't finish that degree in four years. Finish it in eight! So, what? You had a baby out of wedlock. Raise that child and continue to live your life! So, what? Your marriage failed, and you're now divorced. Heal and learn how to love yourself again! God is a God of unlimited chances. He doesn't give up on us, so we don't have permission to give up on ourselves. God holds all power in His hands. He gave us power and dominion over our lives. He gave us an advocate– His spirit. He gave us a sacrificial Lamb, Jesus Christ. He gave us all we need to navigate this thing called life.

If you have lost yourself, now is the time to wake up. Now is the time to be revitalized. Now is the time to see the value in who you are in Christ. Now is the time to answer the call. Now is the time to stand mightily in the victory that God has already won for you. He has done the hard part; all you have to do is walk in it. Now, I realize that sounds easier than it might be in reality, but it is obtainable. You cannot give up on yourself. If no one ever applauds you, I am telling you:

You are a superwoman!

You are valuable!

You are loved!

Someone needs you!

Get up!

Find her again!

Dig deep and give it all you've got!

You can do this, and, honestly, there is nothing and no one stronger than the woman of God you are!

There may be many battles in your life, but those battles are only lost if you give up. Keep fighting. Keep trusting in the undefeatable Father we have. As you continue to fight the battles of life, remember His promise: "God blesses those who patiently endure testing and temptation. Afterward they will receive the crown of life that God has promised to those who love him" (James 1:12, NLT). Find her again and make the life you always wanted.

Let's Pray

Father God,

I thank You for life. No matter what is happening in my life, I will praise You for You are worthy. I have been through so much, and I must admit that life has not been a breeze for me, but I trust You. Forgive me for allowing myself to stray away from You. I want You. I want to be filled again. I want to walk in my calling, and I need You. I realize that I am no one without You. Help me to find myself again. Help me to live out my purpose here on Earth. I desire to be all that You have called me to be, and I will walk in victory in Jesus' name.

I love You. Amen!

What did you miss about yourself most? What new ventures are you planning to explore? What have you learned about yourself in this journey back to you?

I pray that God, the source of hope, will fill you completely with joy and peace because you trust in him. Then you will overflow with confident hope through the power of the Holy Spirit.
Romans 15:13 (NLT)

About the Author

Indigo Manning is a woman of God who seeks to inspire and encourage women through the lens of Christian perspective. She knows and understands how challenging it can be to live a godly life in a world full of other options. This book delves into the biblical tools and applications she used to overcome the many obstacles in her life. Indigo is the wife of Kerry Manning Jr. She is a mother of two boys. She is the daughter of Pastor Lonnie (Felicia) Waller Jr. and LaTrisha (Rico) Newton. She is from the small town of Texarkana, Arkansas, where she graduated from Arkansas High School as an Honor Graduate. She also received a bachelor's degree from Ohio Christian University in English. She is a proud service member of the United States Army, where she has served for ten years. Her sole focus is to serve God in her greatest capacity. Everything she does is for the glory of the Lord! For more of her writing, you can follow her blog full of encouragement and enlightenment at www.violetdeep.org.

Our Motto
"Transforming Life Stories"

Publish Your Book With Us

Our All-Inclusive Self-Publishing Packages
100% Royalties
Professional Proofreading & Editing
Interior Design & Cover Design
Self-Publishing Tutorial & More

For Manuscript Submission or other inquiries:
www.jkenkadepublishing.com
(501) 482-JKEN

Also Available from J. Kenkade Publishing

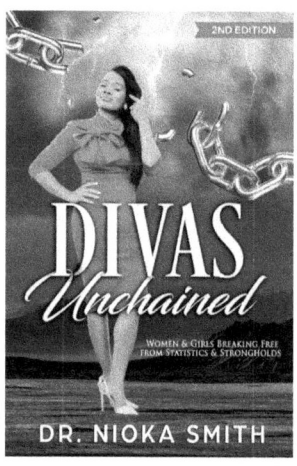

ISBN: 978-1-944486-25-9
Visit www.drniokasmith.com
Author: Dr. Nioka Smith

Sexually abused by her father at the age of 14, pregnant at the age of 17, and a nervous breakdown at the age of 28, Dr. Nioka Smith's painful past almost killed her, until the voice of the Lord guided her into destroying strongholds and reversing Satan's plan for her life. DIVAS Unchained is the powerful chain-breaking reality of the many unfortunate strongholds our women and girls face. Dr. Nioka uses her divine gift to help women and girls break free from destructive life cycles and prosper in all areas of life. Satan has lied to you. It's time to expose his lies. It's time to break free!

Also Available from J. Kenkade Publishing

ISBN: 978-1-944486-90-7
Visit www.amazon.com
Author: Thomas Gray

Marriage by the Book is a profound and practical guidebook designed to help you cultivate a deeper relationship based on sound Biblical wisdom. Written by Pastor Thomas Gray, this book combines proven step-by-step strategies of practical relationships with spiritual lessons and Bible-based principles to help you overcome conflicts, improve your communication, handle difficult discussions, and celebrate the unique union and covenant which unites you together with God. Marriage by the Book is ideal for both new and seasoned couples who are searching for better ways to strengthen their relationship and fulfill their promises to God.

Pastor Thomas Gray: P.O. Box 360041/Dallas, TX 75336
www.twdcdaltx.org (972) 926-3762

Also Available from J. Kenkade Publishing

ISBN: 978-1-944486-51-8
Visit www.amazon.com
Author: Jerry Walker

Do you find yourself asking the question, "Is there more to life than the seemingly never-ending struggle of survival?" This book answers that question with a resounding, "YES!" Jesus died to give us MORE. Jerry Walker has written this manual for Christian living that gives in-depth teaching on scripture and how to apply it to your life. Full of tools for living a life of freedom in Christ, this book will be a blessing to all who read it. Your time is now, it truly is your season!

Also Available from J. Kenkade Publishing

ISBN: 978-1-944486-89-1
Visit www.amazon.com
Author: Machael LaShaunda

Throughout life, we're always confronted with difficulty, but the deftness is learning how to name it, include it, and elevate from it. Studying the story of Judas, I realized it was at the proper time when Jesus rushed Judas away, the betrayal. Though He had the inside scoop on Judas, Jesus gave Judas the same anointing to heal the sick and to go out and teach. Know your Judas, an inspirational testament of the author, is birthed from life encounters and learning how to overcome them. In this book, while reading the pages, it is important to be able to decipher your Judas, so your God given destiny is fulfilled and your purpose is no longer prolonged.

www.ingramcontent.com/pod-product-compliance
Lightning Source LLC
Chambersburg PA
CBHW070203100426
42743CB00013B/3030